THE THIRD JEWEL

I remember wandering around a small reptile and amphibian exhibition several years ago, getting rather tired of table after table of terraria containing corn snakes, rat snakes, and multicolored kingsnakes. Being an amphibian enthusiast, I was disappointed by the seeming delightful little creatures I had ever set eyes on. Unidentified vivid orange frogs the size of my thumbnail with huge soulful eyes seemed unperturbed as I lifted one of the containers. I recall them being extremely expensive at the time, but as I was instantly determined to learn more about

PHOTO: M. STANISZEWSKI.

Their bright colors and general ease of care have made the mantellas popular with hobbyists around the world. This is a female of the Red Golden Mantella, *Mantella aurantiaca rubra*.

deficiency in the frog, toad, newt, and salamander department, but just as I was about to make a well-timed exit I noticed a small and rather non-descript stand tucked away in one dark corner. Scattered around the table, between various herptile volumes and curios, were a few transparent sweater boxes containing some of the most these tiny frogs I ended up taking the entire group of eight. This was my first encounter with the mantellas, and I soon discovered that they were among the most easily kept and beautiful of all the anuran species known to man.

In the eyes of many amphibian enthusiasts mantellas are one of the three "jewels" within the anuran world. The most famous jewel is undoubtedly the Central and South American dendrobatids or poison frogs, whose members often are striking, sometimes brilliant, in coloration. The second "jewel" comprises the less well-known Central American and northern South American frogs called atelopids or harlequin toads, whose species display a bizarre yet stunning array of patterns and colors. The mantellas are equally as colorful and beautifully patterned as the other two and likewise they are small frogs, often measuring less than an inch, and their skin is known to contain toxic alkaloids. They are becoming increasingly fashionable additions to the terrarium, falling somewhere in the middle of the dendrobatids and atelopids in terms of popularity. This is where all similarities end.

Mantellas are distributed in a region of the world thousands of miles from their neotropic cousins: they are found only on the Indian Ocean islands of Madagascar, Reunion, and Seychelles. They are largely diurnal (active during daylight), possibly because these islands possess few predators. Many are mountain-dwellers that can regularly tolerate rather cool temperatures and also are comparatively long-lived for such a small frog. The last and most important fact is that most species have an extremely limited distribution either naturally or due to man's influence. Some species are down to colonies that cover an area of no greater than a

An adult female Beautiful Mantella, *Mantella pulchra*. This is one of the larger species of the genus, with some specimens reaching 30 mm, but as you can see, it is still a tiny frog.

PHOTO: M. STANISZEWSKI.

PHOTO: U. E. FRIESE.

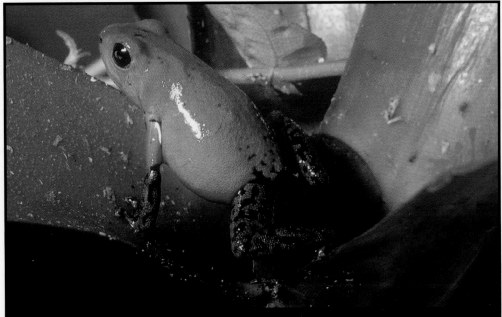

Three groups of small, colorful tropical frogs form the "three jewels" of the terrarium hobby. The poison frogs, Dendrobatidae, of Central and South America perhaps are the best-known of these and the most available. This is the Strawberry Poison Frog, *Dendrobates pumilio*, of Central America.

few hectares. Indeed, the most popular species, the Golden Mantella *(Mantella aurantiaca)*, was appended to the Cites I Endangered animals list during 1994 and now is known from only a handful of localities in central eastern Madagascar. This in turn tells us something else about mantellas—that to be so popular in captivity the sources of most specimens must originate from elsewhere. The answer is that they come to us through captive-breeding, something that has been achieved with all but the most recently discovered species, and even with these it will only be a matter of time.

ABOUT MANTELLAS

The 11 described species (as well as a host of recent and as yet unnamed discoveries) of the genus *Mantella* belong to the huge anuran family Ranidae, the typical frogs, and are currently classed in their own distinct subfamily Mantellinae along with the large and closely related Madagascan arboreal genus *Mantidactylus*. Some experts believe that mantellas are so unique they really deserve family status, and it is not unusual for literature to use the family name Mantellidae. Unlike mantidactylas, mantellas are completely terrestrial frogs, most being rather poor swimmers and climbers, although there are exceptions to these rules. Morphologically-speaking, all species are rather similar and the best method for differentiation is through coloration, although on

An adult female Malagasy Mantella, *Mantella madagascariensis*. Is there any wonder these frogs are considered a jewel in the terrarium crown?

PHOTO: M. STANISZEWSKI.

PHOTO: A. V. D. NIEUWENHUIZEN.

Many mantellas, such as this *Mantella viridis*, have interesting and distinctive throat and belly patterns.

closer study the genus can be split into three distinct groups in terms of distribution, morphology, coloration, and habits. In terms of shape they appear very similar to the typical leopard frogs or European common frogs: the body is slender to slightly plump, the skin is smooth or slightly granular, hind limbs are long and well developed, and the eyes are dark and conspicuous. Unlike their northern counterparts they show a myriad of vivid hues and colors ranging from a coppery brown to a dazzling sky blue, from an iridescent black to a vibrant orange. Such colors are aposematic; that is, they serve to warn potential predators of the dangers in attacking such frogs

whose skin now is known to possess toxic alkaloid secretions similar to some of the dendrobatids. Even more amazing is that some mantellas, such as *Mantella pulchra*, are completely harmless yet have coloring very similar to that of the poisonous species *Mantella madagascariensis*. This is known as Batesian mimicry or "protective coloring."

Mantellas also are among the smallest frogs in the world, with most being in the 15- to 35-mm (0.6 to 1.4 inches) range. Their preferred habitats are the humid floors of mountain forest and woodland, the borders of swamps and pools, and the mossy rock faces of cliffs within the vicinity of spray from waterfalls. However, as their natural habitats continue to diminish through deforestation (75% of the original primary Madagascan forest has been cleared), increased farming, and urban sprawl, a few of the more opportune species are increasingly occurring in lush plantations and even the sewage systems of urban areas. For many species it already may be too late to prevent their extinction in the wild. That is where we, the mantella breeders, come in.

It is envisaged that this book will not only enlighten and endear hobbyists to the increasing number of mantellas now described but also will assist in any attempts made at caring for and breeding these living gems so that they may continue to survive long after wild populations are no more.

PHOTOS: A. V. D. NIEUWENHUIZEN.

Two of the most common mantellas also are among the most attractive. Above is a pair (male the more slender of the two) of the Golden Mantella, *Mantella aurantiaca*. Below is a strikingly marked Malagasy Mantella, *Mantella madagascariensis*.

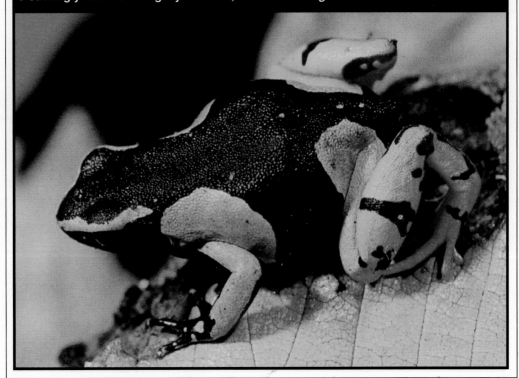

PHOTO: K. H. SWITAK.

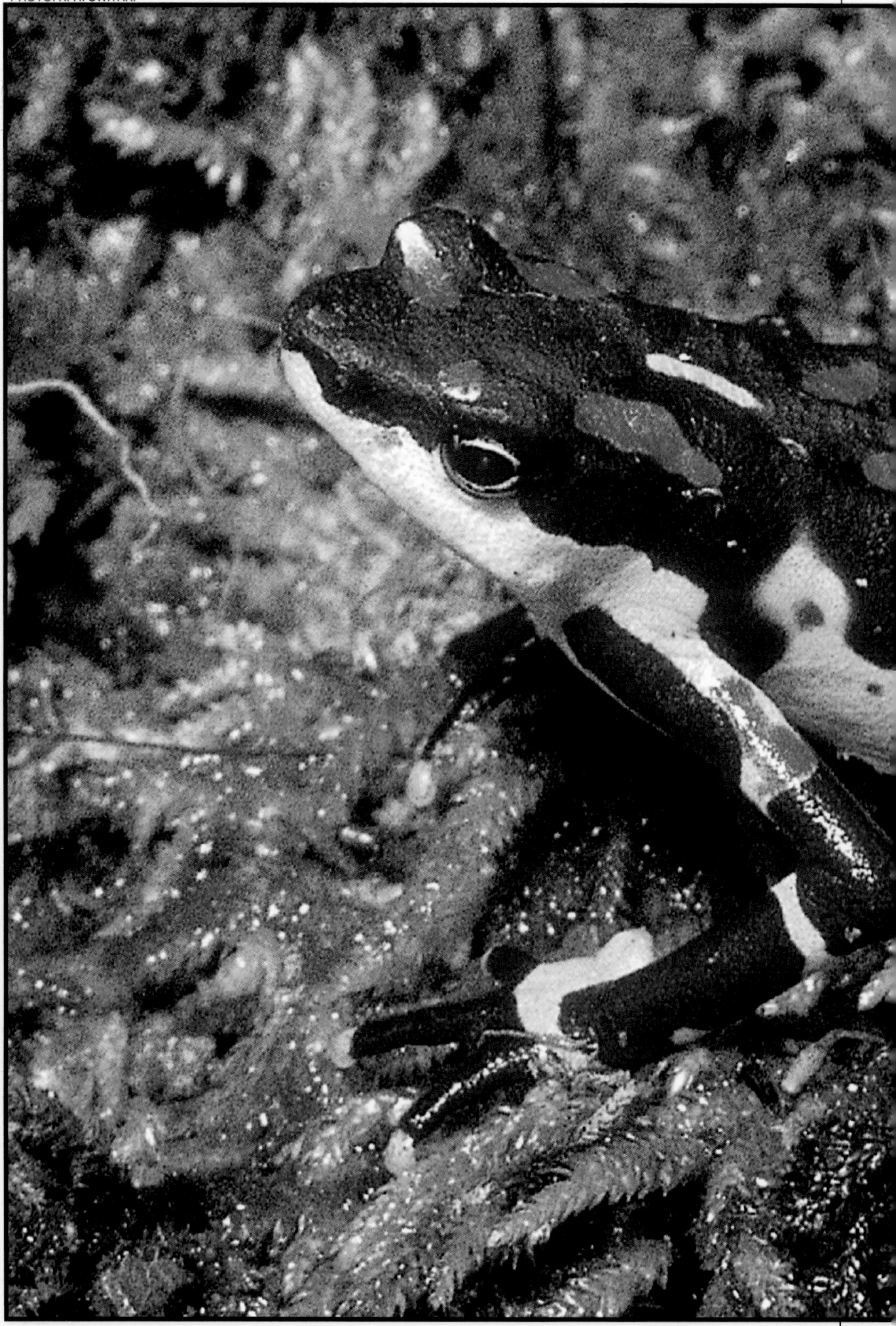

The third jewel of amphibian herpetoculture is the harlequin toads of the genus *Atelopus*. Though many species of this genus are dull and unexciting, some, such as the Central American *Atelopus varius* shown here, are among the most colorful—and difficult—of frogs in captivity.

THE PET MANTELLA

With so little information available on mantellas, plus the fact that until recently only four species—the Golden Mantella *(Mantella aurantiaca)*, Green Mantella *(M. viridis)*, Brown Mantella *(M. betsileo)*, and Cowan's Mantella *(M. cowani)*—had been regularly available, it can be quite a difficult task identifying which types are more suited to the beginner or experienced hobbyist. Data on the habits, habitats, and preferences of many species are quite scarce, and captive husbandry still is in its infancy. One thing that we do know is that if given correct temperatures, humidity, lighting, and varied diets, all species of mantella will not only adapt to captive conditions but actually will thrive in them.

Mantellas, other than the Golden Mantella, are not commonly found for sale in the local pet shop and tropical fish supplier (although it is not unheard of), but the more common species regularly appear in specialist reptile and amphibian pet stores and also on herp pricelists, as does the occasional rarity. Many pet shops will be able to special order the more common mantellas for you from wholesale listings. Regional herp shows and displays may have a few species for sale as well, especially if there are active breeders in the area. Probably the most likely sources of the uncommon species are the offspring from captive breeding programs at zoological societies and especially from mantella hobbyists contacted through herp clubs and associations. In fact, with the latter it is not impossible to locate and obtain every known species of mantella, if you are willing to invest a lot of time and energy in tracking them down.

On establishing the supplier of mantellas, where possible it is

PHOTO: A. V. D. NIEUWENHUIZEN.

A female Golden Mantella, *Mantella aurantiaca*. This certainly is the most commonly available species of the genus at the moment and one of the most striking. Mosses of various types are almost always the basics of mantella husbandry.

PHOTO: W. P. MARA.

Mantellas require relatively cool, humid terraria with many hiding places. Though they are active during the day, they tend to avoid bright lights and may be somewhat reclusive. This attractive *Mantella madagascariensis*, representative of one of the most variable species of the genus, seems at home in these strands of moss.

best to observe specimens before acquisition, especially if they are of a wild-caught source. As with most tropical frogs, individuals inflicted with diseases or injuries survive only long enough for you to buy and relocate into your display terrarium. Ensure that specimens look alert and active, with a healthy, shiny skin free from major damage and eyes and limbs that are intact. Avoid at all costs those that exhibit external parasites such as ticks, usually found around the tympanum (eardrum). In view of the relative expense of these small frogs (1996 list prices of mantellas are in the $30 to $60 range, more for the rarities) such precautions are advisable, although admittedly not always possible.

One final point is the number of mantellas of each species that should be acquired. To observe typical mantella behavior and promote a vigorous breeding colony, at least four specimens are required. Some species are almost impossible to sex, so at least the chances of a sexed pair are higher if a greater number are acquired. Even in easily sexed types such as the Golden Mantella *(M. aurantiaca)* there needs to be some interaction between two territorial males in order to procure a fertile clump of eggs. Sadly, one of each sex rarely equates to a successful breeding.

HANDLING AND QUARANTINE OF MANTELLAS

Due to their small size, mantellas are rather fragile

amphibians and can prove tricky to handle, both during initial transportation and during the cleaning of the terrarium. It is essential that during shipping and also during the trip to your home they are kept sufficiently warm (above 65°F) and moist, because failure to do so can lead to trauma or death. Using small plastic sweater boxes padded with layers of damp kitchen paper or filled with loose sphagnum moss is the best method.

Before releasing them into a terrarium it is wise to keep each specimen in isolation for a period of a week to be certain that they are healthy and are feeding successfully. Failure to do this can result in a "health pyramid" with one or two individuals capturing all the food, gaining in strength, and aggressively defending their territory. The remainder coyly languish in the shadows, gradually becoming stressed out and losing weight, eventually to die. Some species are naturally shy, therefore another important point is to not group socially incompatible types together. The "quarantine" container can consist of just a plastic sweater box with damp kitchen paper that is located in a light and warm (but not hot) position.

Handling mantellas requires gentleness, care, and wet hands. The delicate skin of the mantella can easily be damaged on contact with a warm, dry hand, and most species seem to intensely dislike being disturbed in this way. Therefore handling is best kept to a minimum. Care is particularly recommended in handling poisonous species such as *Mantella aurantiaca* and *M. madagascariensis*, as much discomfort can be experienced if the skin secretions enter an open cut.

In view of some mantellas' agility *(Mantella aurantiaca "milotympanum"* is very nimble), it also is wise to carry out such movements in a fairly open area. Overall it may be wise to simply nudge a frog into a moist plastic beaker and transfer it this way, avoiding handling in any form.

HOUSING MANTELLAS

In their native Madagascar, mantellas occur in three bioclimatically defined terrestrial habitats: lowland evergreen tropical forest; temperate/warm-temperate moist highlands; and dry deciduous woodland. To successfully maintain these amphibians in captivity, such climatic zones must be reflected in the temperature, humidity, lighting, and layout of the terrarium, whether it is to be designed as a natural or simple setup. In addition, there are five basic rules to consider in the husbandry of mantellas that if adhered to will go a long way to ensuring a healthy colony of these delightful frogs:

1. Too small a terrarium will lead to stress.
2. Daytime warmth is appreciated but not hot conditions, while cooler conditions should prevail at night.

3. Humid conditions, but not excessive moisture, are preferred.
4. Good daytime lighting, preferably natural daylight, is essential.
5. Ensure that the terrarium and its contents are regularly cleaned out.

reserved only for effectively rearing juvenile mantellas as described later in the book.

In the main, mantella species tend to be rather bold and inquisitive and thus can be maintained in a glass aquarium providing it has undergone a few minor adjustments. Commercial

PHOTO: W. P. MARA.

An underview of the Black-eared Mantella, *Mantella aurantiaca "milotympanum,"* adhering to the glass. Do not be misled that these terrestrial frogs can't climb—the terrarium should be covered to prevent escapes and also to control humidity.

Types of Terraria

Before deciding on the layout, the type of terrarium container and its size must first be considered. I have known someone to successfully maintain and breed the Yellow Mantella (*Mantella crocea*) in a plastic shoe box filled with damp moss. However, this is an exception to the rule. Such a container provides the hobbyist with little scope to observe these fascinating frogs' behavior and so are better

aquarium background scenes should be affixed to the sides and the rear of the aquarium; they will not only enhance the terrarium but also reduce snout injuries from mantellas attempting to leap through the glass. Needless to say, the top of the terrarium must be fitted with a secure lid because with the aid of moisture these small frogs can easily use their belly as a sucker to scale the smooth glass sides.

Mantellas such as *Mantella*

haraldmeieri, *Mantella aurantiaca* "milotympanum," and *Mantella pulchra* are shy, jumpy, and easily stressed species better off housed in a glass-fronted wooden terrarium. The enclosed nature of this design provides them with a little more security, thus they will settle down and exist in captivity much more successfully.

Size of Terrarium

Even though mantellas are small frogs, this does not mean that they will be content with a small container. On the contrary, adult mantellas of both sexes often are highly territorial and prefer to energetically defend a small area. Too small a container will almost certainly promote stress due to excessive fighting or even complete break-down of the territorial hierarchy, something that should be avoided if a serious attempt at breeding these frogs is to be made. With all species being in the 15- to 35-mm range, for a typical colony of between four and eight adult mantellas the terrarium size range should be 24 to 36 inches long, 12 to 15 inches deep, and 12 to 18 inches wide. Anything bigger than this and interaction between individuals will be almost non-existent, and again breeding potential is likely to decrease.

Layout and Design

The layout is an important factor in the successful husbandry of mantellas although it does not necessarily have to be of a complicated design. First of all, the natural habitat of the species to be kept must be considered; i.e., the

three bioclimatic habitat bands into which a species falls. The design then can be sculpted around this. Some species, such as *Mantella madagascariensis*, occur in all three habitats, and therefore it may be wise to discover roughly where new acquisitions originated. Alternatively, if they are of a captive-bred source, try to ascertain the conditions under which the parents were maintained.

Natural Setups

Although natural setups are pleasing to the eye and can become the focal point of any room, it must be understood that they will require much attention and are not essential in the successful maintenance and breeding of mantellas. Mantella setups demand being thoroughly cleaned once a week mainly because of the large amounts of droppings, which will quickly show fungal growth in the humid atmosphere these frogs require. Natural terraria must reflect the habitat preferences of the species they are to contain.

• **Species Hailing from Tropical Evergreen Lowland Forest**
(*M. bernhardi, M. cowani, M. crocea, M. haraldmeieri, M. laevigata, M. madagascariensis, M. "marojezyi"*)

The emphasis should be on plenty of decorative bog wood, pieces of bark, small rocks draped with mosses, small plants such as those ferns, ivies, marantas, and others frequently used in horticultural bottle gardens, along

PHOTO: M. STANISZEWSKI.

A simple but attractive hygienic setup for keeping mantellas.

with a small shallow water source. Plants should be located so that most of the base, which can consist of a mixture of sphagnum/Java moss, twigs, leaves, and bark chips, is partially shaded from the light source. This type of terrarium must be lightly misted three or four times daily with luke-warm water.

- **Species Hailing from Temperate/Warm-temperate Moist Highland Forest**

(*M. aurantiaca, M. betsileo, M. aurantiaca "milotympanum," M. pulchra, M. "loppei," M. madagascariensis, M. "marojezyi"*)

These species enjoy skulking around in leaf litter but also defend exposed, often dry

positions such as large rocks and tree stumps. The emphasis is on the slightly lower nighttime temperatures and sparser plant life to give an overall well-lit base. This should consist of shredded moss and bark chips as well as a few flat rocks such as slate. A large rock or lump of bog wood should either be centrally positioned or located to one side of the terrarium. A shallow water pan should be positioned away from the light source. This type of terrarium must be well misted twice daily with luke-warm water.

- **Species Hailing from Dry Deciduous Forest**

(*M. betsileo, M. expectata, M. viridis, M. madagascariensis*)

In the wild these mantellas

Madagascar continues to yield surprises, such as this so-far undescribed bright red mantella commonly called *Mantella aurantiaca "milotympanum."* Undescribed species often are imported for the terrarium hobby before scientists get to them.

PHOTO: M. STANISZEWSKI.

PHOTO: M. STANISZEWSKI.

The Yellow Mantella, *Mantella crocea*, hails from tropical evergreen forests in the Madagascan lowlands.

often are found in the vicinity of brooks or small bodies of water within dry lowland forest (especially in western Madagascar), particularly in and around rocks and debris that either receive spray from coursing water or are partially submerged to soak up moisture. Such mantellas also will venture into drier areas in search of invertebrates, therefore the terrarium is best divided into "dryish" (given an occasional light spray) and damp. The dry area should consist of bark chips, twigs, and rocks, while the damp zone should contain a shallow water pan surrounded by rocks and bog wood padded out with sphagnum moss. This type of terrarium must be lightly misted three or four times daily with luke-warm water.

Simple (Hygienic) Setups

After successfully keeping and breeding mantellas for many years, I can say with some confidence that a hygienic or simple setup is just as successful as those natural styles defined above. Moreover, it is far easier to maintain and healthier for the frogs. The secret is to attempt to imitate the natural style terraria using mainly synthetic products (with the exception of natural rocks, logs, and small sections of moss) that are widely available at pet and tropical fish stores.

Misting frequencies are in line with natural terraria to achieve suitably humid conditions.

- **Species Hailing from Tropical Evergreen Lowland Forest**

(*M. bernhardi, M. cowani, M. crocea, M. haraldmeieri, M. laevigata, M. madagascariensis, M. "marojezyi"*)

The base should be of a spongy, absorbent material that is able to hold moisture. Kitchen paper or folded layers of cotton material are suitable; however, synthetic sponge or foam rubber as used in upholstery is ideal if thoroughly washed prior to use. Attempt to acquire a dark color such as green or brown that suitably matches the mossy floor of a forest. A circle can be cut into the foam to allow a shallow water dish to be sunk, although this should always be away from the light source. An attractive piece of bog wood can be centrally located and pieces of curved cork bark, ceramic logs or rocks, and leaves of imitation plants made out of acrylic or nylon should be freely scattered on top of the foam to provide plenty of humid hiding places. To gain the overall effect of Madagascan rainforest, locate several long branches of the imitation plants to give the impression of a sheltered forest floor. Not only will these help to subdue the light source, but they also will increase humidity near the base. The beauty of such a setup is that the whole lot can be washed and used many times.

- **Species Hailing from Temperate/Warm-temperate Moist Highland Forest**

(*M. aurantiaca, M. betsileo, M. aurantiaca "milotympanum," M. pulchra, M. "loppei," M. madagascariensis, M. "marojezyi"*)

The same setup as described above is required, but there should be fewer or no overhead plants and more small rocks should be scattered on top of the foam base. Exposed, dry positions such as large rocks and bog wood stumps should be evident. An ample shallow water pan should be positioned into the foam away from the light source or path of sunlight.

- **Species Hailing from Dryish Deciduous Forest**

(*M. betsileo, M. expectata, M. viridis, M. madagascariensis*)

The base should be divided into two, one half consisting of the damp foam while the other half should be a drier material such as the soft synthetic turf used by fruit sellers or the grass matting currently being manufactured specifically for herptiles and invertebrates. (Astroturf is not acceptable as its plastic grass blades cause discomfort in these frogs.) Again, a shallow water pan should be sunk half into the synthetic turf, half into the foam and encircled by plenty of rocks, bog wood pieces, and porcelain logs. Both areas should be freely scattered with imitation plant leaves and cork bark, while small cubes of damp foam and sponge should pad out the rocks and logs on the damper side to recreate natural caves.

Other Points of Note

In all three simple style setups

it is essential to allocate one corner of the terrarium for nesting. About 4 square inches of the substrate should be removed and replaced with a constantly damp area consisting of a loose material into which mantellas can burrow. I have tried many artificial products such as tissue shallow water dishes no deeper than 2 inches (preferably to 1 inch is recommended) and with easy access and egression points are best. A piece of slate sloping into the water along with a bunch of partially submerged waterweed (real or plastic depending on style chosen), for instance, works well.

PHOTO: M. STANISZEWSKI.

The Black-eared Mantella, *Mantella aurantiaca "milotympanum,"* is immediately recognizable by the rough skin and black nostril and tympanum.

paper, cotton linen, cotton wool, and finely chopped pieces of sponge with varying degrees of success. Live sphagnum or Java moss has consistently proved more fruitful for nesting as described in more detail in the breeding section.

A final point is that although many mantellas enjoy bathing they are not as aquatic as other ranids, with some species being very poor swimmers. Therefore

Heat and Light

Perhaps the most fascinating aspect of these frogs is their similarity of behavior with another Madagascan herptile—day geckos of the genus *Phelsuma*. Like the day geckos, every single species is diurnal (although some are known to forage at night), a feature that goes against the grain where most amphibians are concerned. Obviously this makes for a highly interesting and conspicuous terrarium subject—but only if the temperature and lighting are suitable.

• **Heat**

Madagascar lies below the equator within the tropics, but because it is such a large island temperatures tend to vary widely through each bioclimatic habitat. The lowland evergreen rainforests on the eastern side of the island experience the most consistent daily and seasonal temperatures, while the highland areas show the greatest shifts. Although different species of mantella demand different optimum temperature ranges, they all are capable of withstanding relatively cool nighttime temperatures. However, correct thermoregulation plays an extremely important role in reproduction regimes, so it is in the best interests of the hobbyist to attempt to provide optimum conditions accordingly. In my own experience few mantella species enjoy temperatures above 85°F and tend to disappear under bark, into moss, or beneath rocks when the temperature rises past this level. However, in their native Madagascar such phenomena occur naturally, particularly in the west in drier deciduous forests, therefore such species are only openly active after dawn and before dusk for several hours in each case. Those species from the highlands such as *Mantella aurantiaca* can endure temperatures on average 5 to 15°F cooler and often are active for 90% of the daylight hours.

Generally speaking, mantellas dislike a source of intense projected heat such as a spot or other reflector lamp, therefore heating is best achieved via other means. One of the best methods is to locate the terrarium in a room that normally is at room temperature (approximately 68°F) and then use a "dull heat emitter," i.e., a heater with a low surface temperature, to boost the air temperature to the required level. Under-terrarium heater pads or mats, plastic-coated heating strips or cables, or even low-wattage microceramic units now are manufactured specifically for herptiles. A thermostat is essential in maintaining correct temperatures; the sensor should be located half buried or resting on the surface of the basal substrate.

The preferred temperature ranges for each bioclimatic habitat zone are as follows:

Tropical Evergreen Lowland Forest:

Cool Season (May to Sept.)*: 66 to 70°F nighttime, 70 to 80°F daytime

Warm Season (Oct. to April): 68 to 72°F nighttime; 72 to 85°F daytime

Temperate/Warm-temperate Highlands:

Cool Season: 62 to 70°F nighttime; 66 to 75°F daytime

Warm Season: 65 to 70°F nighttime; 68 to 76°F daytime

Dry Deciduous Forest:

Cool Season: 62 to 75°F nighttime; 68 to 78°F daytime

Warm Season: 70 to 75°F nighttime; 74 to 86°F daytime

(*These temperatures apply to Southern Hemisphere

Though not colorful, Bernhard's Mantella, *Mantella bernhardi*, is one of those rare species that specialists live for. It seldom has been bred in captivity.

(Madagascan) conditions. Of course, in the Northern Hemisphere these seasons can be switched to take advantage of the naturally warmer weather conditions occurring from May to October, although in terms of breeding wild-caught mantellas it may take a year to two to adjust them.)

• **Lighting**

Photoperiod (hours of light per day) is not as critical as with those amphibians hailing from temperate zones. Gradually reducing photoperiod from 16 hours in the middle of the warm season to around 12 hours during the cool season should suffice. The type of lighting can be influential where the breeding potential of a mantella colony in captivity is concerned. **Tungsten or incandescent lighting** in the form of a bulb or small strip light is the most economical, with a 25 to 40 watt bulb being required. This should be located to one side of the terrarium (at the opposite end from the water dish) so that there is a gradual thermal gradient that allows overheated mantellas to escape to the cool area and vice versa. Such lighting is suitable only for those terraria lacking live plants and will give limited success where breeding mantellas is concerned, mainly with the shyer or less active species such as *Mantella aurantiaca "milotympanum"* and *Mantella pulchra*.

Ultraviolet (UV) lighting in the form of fluorescent tubes is undoubtedly the most successful type of illumination in the mantella terrarium, particularly for the more showy species such as *M. aurantiaca*, *M. viridis*, and *M. bernhardi*. Being largely diurnal, mantellas are one of the few amphibians to benefit from the ultraviolet transmission of balanced natural daylight lamps. Not only does this light possess germicidal properties, but it also assists in the mobilization and synthesis of vitamin D3, phosphorus, and calcium, all essential in maintaining a healthy appetite and skeletal and skin growth. Also worth noting is that such lighting emits only a small amount of heat, therefore the terrarium will not "cook" under warm ambient conditions outside the terrarium. Additionally, UV light helps plants to flourish in planted terraria and significantly enhances the display terrarium. UV spot lamp reflectors such as blacklight and reflectorized UVA also are available, but because of the heat these give out they are not really suitable for mantellas.

One final aspect of lighting is the utilization of timer switches and rheostats. Combined units allow an exact photoperiod to be set and the gradual dimming of the light source to prevent mantellas suddenly being cast into darkness. However, such units are rather expensive so simply switching on a main room light before manually switching off the terrarium light source is just as effective.

Terrarium Maintenance

Unlike many anurans that tend to locate a water source to defecate, mantellas are rather indiscriminate in this respect, and therefore the terrarium can become soiled very quickly. Warm, humid conditions will quickly promote fungal and bacterial growth that, if left unchecked, can prove disastrous in such a small environment. With this in mind, a complete cleaning out of the terrarium is recommended on a weekly basis and certainly no longer than every two weeks. Of course with a natural setup this can prove very time-consuming, with the basal substrate having to be thoroughly washed or changed (quite a messy task), live plants wiped down, and all other decor items washed. In the simple terrarium the substrate, imitation plants, and all other decor need only be thoroughly rinsed in hot water. The terrarium itself will need to be washed down with a proprietary household disinfectant and then thoroughly swilled out with clean water.

FEEDING MANTELLAS

Mantellas are exclusively insectivorous frogs using a long sticky tongue to snare a wide variety of small arachnids, insects, and other invertebrates. Some species, such as *Mantella haraldmeieri*, have rather fastidious preferences, feeding only on a small variety of invertebrates, which sometimes

Temperature seems to be the major influencing factor in determining the appetite of the mantella. Too cool (or to a lesser extent too warm) results in food being refused or food that was previously eaten being regurgitated. Maintaining mantellas at the temperatures recommended earlier should

PHOTO: M. STANISZEWSKI.

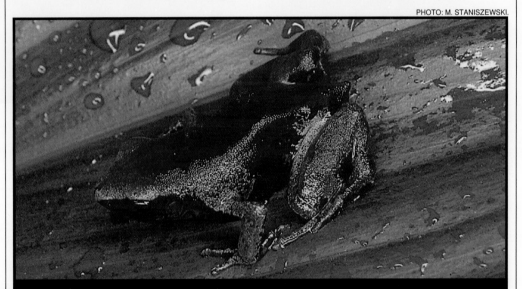

A male Beautiful Mantella, *Mantella pulchra*. Tiny frogs need tiny food, so the mantella keeper must be able to provide a varied diet of tiny crickets, fruitflies, and other insects on a continuing basis.

can present difficulties if such foods are in short supply. Other species, such as *M. aurantiaca* and *M. madagascariensis*, can eventually be coaxed into taking most of the food types offered by livefood suppliers plus some surprising additions and should present problems only when other aspects of their husbandry are neglected.

negate such problems. Newly acquired mantellas may refuse food for the first few days, although I have seen this occur only in *M. bernhardi, M. haraldmeieri, M. "marojezyi," and M. pulchra.*

In the wild, mantellas spend much of their time foraging for invertebrates beneath leaves on the forest floor. In captivity this can be mirrored only to a certain extent because in the interests of hygiene it is not wise to have a terrarium where prey is running around continually. Restrict feeding to two or three small offerings each day; one in the morning, one in the afternoon, and one in the evening prior to the lights being switched off. Each feeding should consist of perhaps two to six individual items per mantella. In addition, offering a wide variety of invertebrates will go a long way to maintaining a healthy colony and thus increasing breeding potential.

FOOD TYPES

The types of prey listed below are not exhaustive, and the hobbyist is admonished to offer as wide a variety as possible. Some foods are seasonal only, while some are available only in certain parts of the world. The list has been split up into three categories: commercially available, wild-caught, and alternative foods and supplements.

Commercially Available Foods
- **Crickets**
  These are the most practical

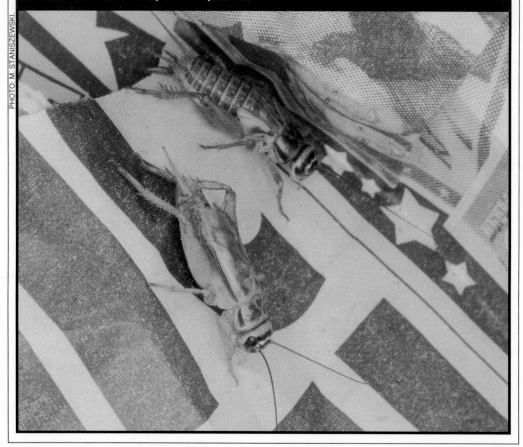

Crickets, especially the commonly bred *Acheta domesticus*, will form the basis of the mantella diet. Winged adults are too large for most mantellas, but their tiny offspring are excellent food and easily bred or purchased.

PHOTO: M. STANISZEWSKI.

PHOTO: M. STANISZEWSKI.

Portrait of a common cricket, *Acheta domesticus*. This immature female (notice the large wing pads and the obvious but blunt ovipositor) probably is too large for any but the largest and most aggressively feeding mantellas.

and favored food for captive mantellas, and even the most fussy species can eventually be persuaded to take them, although *Mantella haraldmeieri* is sometimes the exception. Three types currently are available from livefood suppliers: the Brown House Cricket *(Acheta domesticus)*; the Black Field Cricket *(Gryllus* sp.*)*, and the Silent Cricket *(Gryllus assimilis)*, all of which are recommended, although the Black Field Crickets in particular are relished. For the adults of most species, only crickets within the 2- to 5-mm size range should be offered, although adult *M. madagascariensis* and *M. pulchra* can devour crickets of 8 to 10mm in size. To increase the nutritional value of crickets it is wise to feed them on a moist, crumbly mixture of bran and chopped carrot fortified with a multivitamin supplement prior to feeding to the mantellas. This is known as gut-loading.

- **Fruitflies**

Most mantellas seem to enjoy fruitflies, although *Mantella bernhardi* and *M. aurantiaca* "*milotympanum*" occasionally will refuse them. Cultures of these small (1 to 2mm) flies are available from livefood suppliers. Purchased flies can either be immediately utilized as food or some of them (around 20 to 30) can be transferred to fresh cultures consisting of yeast and mashed apple or banana fortified with a liquid multivitamin supplement. Until recently the vestigial-winged form of

Drosophila melanogaster was the most commonly available fruitfly, but currently a larger (2 to 3mm) fully-winged but flightless Trinidadian species is fast becoming a favorite. Both types are suitable, but be warned that the vestigial-winged form can sometimes revert to a fully flighted fly.

• **Waxworms (Honey Worms)**

The larvae of the Honey Moth *(Galleria mellonella)* sold by livefood suppliers tend to be too large for mantellas to consume, although hatchling larvae are suitable. Recently Lesser Waxmoth larvae *(Achroia grisella)* have appeared on the market, and at 2 to 5mm these are an excellent source of nutrition. Unfortunately not all mantellas enjoy them, possibly because of the hairy epidermis or the slight odor emitted. It is quite amusing to see a mantella eject a Lesser Waxworm from its mouth then trail its long tongue along the ground to wipe away the taste. Only *M. aurantiaca, M. expectata, M. laevigata, M. madagascariensis, M. pulchra,* and *M. viridis* will avidly take them, but all is not lost; the larvae can be allowed to develop into the small moths that will then be greedily devoured by all mantellas.

• **Mealworms**

Smaller larvae (3 to 8mm) of the

A newly hatched grasshopper. European hobbyists often can purchase captive-bred locusts (a type of grasshopper) at tiny sizes. These make a nice change of pace for feeding mantellas.

PHOTO: M. STANISZEWSKI.

PHOTO: M. STANISZEWSKI.

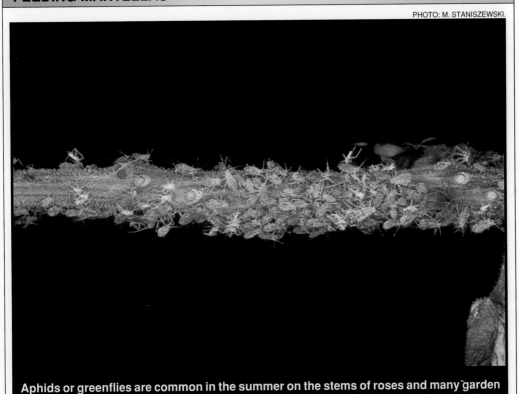

Aphids or greenflies are common in the summer on the stems of roses and many garden plants. If a stem of the plant carrying their colonies is put with the mantellas, the frogs quickly will find them and begin a feeding frenzy.

flour beetle *Tenebrio molitor* occasionally are taken by less fussy species, although I would always recommend using freshly molted mealworms, distinguished by their milky white appearance.

Wild-caught Foods

One important consideration if utilizing invertebrates caught in the garden or countryside is to make sure they have not come into contact with pesticides or herbicides that may harm or even kill frogs as small as mantellas. Also, there is always a chance of introducing a parasite or pathogen into a mantella colony, although I have never known this to happen in ten years of maintaining these frogs.

- **Ants & Termites**

   In the wild, some mantellas, especially *M. haraldmeieri*, feed exclusively on ants and termites. However, the small black and red ants typical to Northern Hemisphere gardens seem to be very distasteful, while termites are difficult to locate. Summer flying ants are occasionally devoured, as are wood ants.

- **Sweepings**

   Brushing a fine mesh net through a meadow in spring or summer will yield a wide variety of springtails, flies, spiders, and other invertebrates. Nutritionally this represents the best food type.

- **Aphids (including greenfly, blackfly, cabbagefly & whitefly)**

PHOTO: M. STANISZEWSKI.

Bloodworms can be tried as an alternative food for mantellas. If put into a small cup with a minimum of water, their wriggling may attract the attention of the frogs. They also may be taken by froglets.

An excellent source of nutritional food in spring and summer, aphids often congregate on roses, bramble, nettles, and vegetables. A whole branch snipped off and placed in the terrarium will provide mantellas with many hours of enjoyment as they pick off stray aphids. They are taken by all mantellas, even *M. haraldmeieri.*

- **Beetles**

Beetles are a common prey for wild mantellas, and the small black groundbeetles are taken by most species.

- **Earthworms**

Small chopped earthworms are taken by *M. aurantiaca* and *M. viridis* but should be thoroughly washed prior to feeding. Cut the earthworm into 5- to 10-mm strips.

Other foods such as fleshflies, millipedes, centipedes, small woodlice, gnats, mosquitoes, caterpillars, small moths, and small spiders all can be offered occasionally to give as much variety as possible.

Alternative Foods and Supplements

Mantella aurantiaca is the most adaptable species in terms of food types, and I have found this species to regularly accept small pieces of raw lean meat from the end of forceps. Although not a necessary food, it is excellent for sustaining the frog's weight if the hobbyist is unable to offer food for several days. *M. viridis* and *M. madagascariensis* also will occasionally take meat.

Proprietary multivitamin supplement in powder form can be dusted onto foods to provide the mantellas with the correct levels of vitamins and trace elements. If a variety of foods is regularly offered, then a multivitamin powder is only necessary every third or fourth meal, but during winter when wild-caught foods become scarce it is recommended at least every other meal. There is evidence to suggest that such supplements increase the breeding potential of mantellas.

BREEDING MANTELLAS

Fortunately, mantellas are one of those few amphibians that will breed even when conditions are not perfect. Yellow Mantellas (*M. crocea*) have been bred in a plastic shoe box filled with damp sphagnum moss. However, such a container gives the hobbyist little opportunity to observe the complex, absorbing, and often amusing behavior of these beautiful frogs prior to and during egg deposition. Reproduction occurs up to ten times throughout the year in eastern and northern lowland and central highland Madagascan species. Those hailing from the drier western and southwestern regions tend to have a roughly defined breeding season from October to April, producing up to four clutches of eggs.

Males and females are highly territorial and will attempt to guard their small domain by nudging and wrestling intruders away. Males often will vociferate with a series of short, high-pitched calls that sound much like a loud cricket. Oddly, *Mantella aurantiaca* "*milotympanum*' is far more vociferous than the more showy *M. aurantiaca*, sometimes calling for hours on end! Besides defending a territory, males (and occasionally females) will attempt to entice the opposite sex with a display of vocalization (males only), dancing, and clasping. Such behavior is likely to occur in captivity following a misting or feeding period when the movement and foraging seem to

A typical egg clutch of the Golden Mantella, *Mantella aurantiaca*, laid in a protected spot in the sphagnum.

PHOTO: M. STANISZEWSKI.

induce excitement in these frogs. A female will be receptive only if egg deposition is imminent, then allowing the male to clasp her. Mantellas are one of the few anuran genera to display three types of amplexus: around the head (known as cephalic amplexus); just behind the forearms (axillary amplexus); and in front of the hind limbs (inguinal amplexus). If she accepts the male's advances she will then carry him to a dark, moist location (often in a cave, hole, or mossy excavation near the water source). There are few better sights than cleaning out a terrarium only to discover a small clump of eggs nestled in some sphagnum moss beneath a damp log or attached to a stone overlapping the water dish. Unfortunately, it also is quite common for the female to deposit a clutch of eggs that are not subsequently fertilized.

Sexing Mantellas (Sexual Dimorphism)

In an ideal situation, to promote a more vigorous pairing two or three males are required for every female. Unfortunately a successful pairing rarely takes place when there is only one of

Female mantellas, like this *Mantella aurantiaca*, carry large eggs and may appear very plump a few days before laying.

PHOTO: M. STANISZEWSKI

PHOTO: M. STANISZEWSKI.

A male (notice the slender shape) Golden Mantella, *Mantella aurantiaca*, guarding an egg clutch. The parents often return to the eggs to spray them with water from the bladder to assure they stay moist.

each sex, although it is not unheard of. To the beginner and sometimes even the expert, sexing mantellas can prove quite daunting because externally both sexes appear very similar. In some species sexual dimorphism is very obvious, while in others only by studying mantellas for some time can the subtle differences between the female and male be gauged. Sexual dimorphism for each species is discussed in more detail in the species section later, but at least a few general conclusions can be drawn here.

Males sometimes can be determined immediately from their calling (I have never been into a herp shop where at least one male is not happily chirruping), but quite often non-calling males are misinterpreted as females. Males generally are smaller, more streamlined, have a more angular and smaller head, and often are more brightly colored than females. However, small females may be misinterpreted as full-grown males.

Males of some species have more distinct femoral glands (colored patches on either side of the vent). These glands are thought to be used by rubbing against the female to arouse her into egg-laying, but in some species the females also possess femoral glands.

In the males of species that lack the dark pigmentation on the ventral surface (i.e., *M. aurantiaca*, some *M. crocea*, and *M. a.* "milotympanum"), a pair of thin white lines is sometimes visible through the semi-transparent belly. These are known as seminiferous or sperm ducts. They have a dual function: in addition to transporting sperm they also carry urine and are therefore also called ureters. They run from the cloaca to the middle of the belly. In females the pair of ureters (obviously females do not possess sperm ducts) is in the same position but is concealed behind the oviducts and related structures and therefore is not visible.

Alternative Reproductive Stimuli

Besides the incidence of defined seasons playing a part in the reproductive cycle of mantellas of the drier western regions of Madagascar, mantellas of all species sometimes can be induced to breed by other methods in captivity. Often such conditions do not naturally arise in the wild, and the degree of success varies for each species.

Although not naturally occurring in dry regions, *Mantella*

Day four finds some of the eggs in this Golden Mantella clutch already developing into tadpoles with straight tails.

PHOTO: M. STANISZEWSKI.

PHOTO: M. STANISZEWSKI.

Some mantellas, such as the Green Mantella, *Mantella viridis*, are very difficult to breed in captivity. Possibly they suffer from a vitamin or mineral deficiency, as heavy dusting of the food with a multivitamin powder has led to limited successes in the terrarium.

aurantiaca and to a lesser extent *M. betsileo* can be stimulated into courtship and egg-laying by allowing the terrarium to dry out for a period of two to four weeks. Water must still be made accessible in the form of a shallow dish, and the whole setup should be lightly misted in the morning to imitate dew, but otherwise normal spraying regimes are withheld. At the end of the dry period, the terrarium should be thoroughly misted until any depressions partially fill up with water. This may encourage males to call vigorously, and if the normal spraying regime is carried out, mating should occur within the next four to six weeks.

The Green Mantella *(M. viridis)* is perhaps one of the most difficult mantellas to breed in captivity. Females often develop eggs and males call frequently, yet couplings rarely take place. Even in the wild it is not an especially common species, being confined to a few localized habitats where it seems to breed only once or twice per year. After various experiments I had success by feeding Green Mantellas with prey heavily dusted in multivitamin powder. In addition, this species appears to dislike competing with other mantella species for food and territory. Perhaps it is a chemical within the multivitamin powder that triggers mating, because these mantellas feed almost exclusively on beetles and termites in Madagascar. Success with such supplements also has been documented for *M. madagascariensis* and *M. cowani.*

In highland species the advent of a "cool" season certainly plays a part in stimulating courtship. Maintaining a temperature of 65 to 70°F for six to eight weeks during autumn or winter, with a slight drop at night, will still keep the mantellas active although their food intake will be smaller. Gradually increasing the temperature to their preferred optimum levels can encourage frenzied courtship dancing, wrestling, and territorial displays during which females develop eggs. If you are lucky a successful pairing will then ensue.

Egg Deposition, Development, and Care

Mantellas are one of those unusual genera that lay their eggs on land. Initial development takes place within the egg capsule until the tadpoles are washed out by heavy rain or squirm out into nearby pools.

In captivity female mantellas do not seem to be as particular in their choice of egg-laying sites as mantellas in the wild. As long as the location is moist, protected, and relatively dark they seem quite content. This location can be in the form of the underside of a piece of bark or broken crock, squeezed down the side of a water bowl, or, in the case of *Mantella laevigata*, holes or chambers in elevated sections of hollow bamboo. However, damp moss in

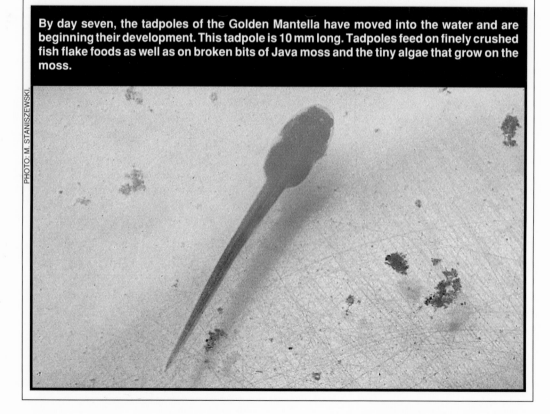

By day seven, the tadpoles of the Golden Mantella have moved into the water and are beginning their development. This tadpole is 10 mm long. Tadpoles feed on finely crushed fish flake foods as well as on broken bits of Java moss and the tiny algae that grow on the moss.

PHOTO: M. STANISZEWSKI.

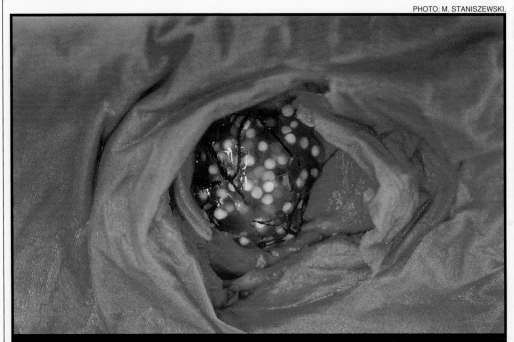

PHOTO: M. STANISZEWSKI.

A freshly laid egg clutch of the Yellow Mantella, *Mantella crocea*. In captivity females are not choosy about where they lay as long as it is moist and secluded. This clutch was laid in a wad of damp paper towels.

whatever shape or form is almost always chosen. Females excavate a depression in the moss with their hind limbs before depositing a round or slightly oblong clump containing 10 to 100 eggs depending on the age, size, and species of the mantella concerned. The egg nucleus or pole usually is unpigmented or pale in color (gray, yellow, sand, or green) and measures between 1 and 2mm across. It is surrounded by a clear or slightly opaque gelatinous covering measuring a total of 3 to 5mm in diameter. If the eggs are fertile, evidence of embryonic development can be seen in the first two or three days. Batches of infertile eggs commonly are seen and will either collapse or become cloudy and shrink in the first three to five days. At this point it

is best to remove the eggs, which will also begin to smell. For fertile eggs, as the embryo begins to form the egg absorbs moisture and swells. Quite often both sexes will tend to the eggs by discharging fluid over them, especially in dry conditions. I had a male Golden Mantella that "guarded" the eggs for the whole duration until the tadpoles hatched out.

I have found no reason to remove the eggs from the terrarium in the initial stages for the simple reason that parental attention may prove imperative in successful embryo development. Eggs removed immediately after laying may even fail to develop. Certainly eggs should never be immediately transferred to water, as this will result in instant death of the embryo. After two to seven days, however, it is recommended to transfer the eggs, disturbing them as little as possible. At this stage the general tadpole shape will be very evident and provisions for their entrance to an aquatic world will need to be made. I have found that placing the eggs on a mossy platform that slopes gently into a shallow body of water within an aquarium is the best method. This allows the 6- to 10-mm tadpoles the opportunity to slide or wriggle safely into the water after 4 to 14 days. The air temperature should be consistent with that in the adult terrarium.

Tadpole Development and Care

A 24-inch aquarium with 2 to 5 inches of boiled and then cooled slightly acidic water (i.e., rainwater, provided it is largely free of pollutants and toxins—mantella tadpoles are known to be slightly tolerant of polluted, stagnant, and eutrophic water) will prove ideal for up to 80 tadpoles. The water should be gently aerated and filtered, with a gravel bottom. Live submerged and floating plants should be abundant, while the water temperature should be within the range of 66 to 74°F. Tadpoles develop quite quickly and are almost entirely herbivorous,

A large clutch of eggs of the Beautiful Mantella, *Mantella pulchra*, laid in a hole in a tree limb. Remember, the exact laying site is not as important as that it is moist and hidden from view.

PHOTO: M. STANISZEWSKI.

A pretty, newly metamorphosed froglet of Bernhard's Mantella, *Mantella bernhardi*. This froglet is only 5 mm long, thus the obvious need for tiny living foods. Notice that the colors and pattern are somewhat different from those of the adults.

filter-feeding on algae growing on the gravel, plants, or sides of the aquarium or on detritus suspended or floating on the surface. Gradually they develop rasp-like pseudoteeth and beaky mouthparts that are used to tear away vegetable matter. Alternatively they can be offered vitamin-enriched fish pellets when they are over 30 days old. Given a healthy diet, idyllic conditions, and regular partial water changes (a third of the water removed and replaced with fresh pre-boiled rainwater every seven days), after 40 to 70 days tadpoles will have reached a maximum mouth to tail tip length of about 30mm, depending on the species. At this stage the hind limbs will be well-developed and the forelimbs will begin to break through. The tadpole then begins to absorb its tail and spends more and more time at the surface. Easily accessible islands consisting of mossy sloping rocks must be made available, and the water level can be gradually lowered to about 1 to 1.5 inches. After 45 to 100 days the 5- to 8-mm froglets, which appear nothing like their parents in terms of coloration, will emerge.

PHOTO: M. STANISZEWSKI.

A newly metamorphosed Golden Mantella, *Mantella aurantiaca*, looks nothing like the adult. It may take two months or more before the full adult coloration is assumed.

Froglet Care

To prevent drowning, mantella froglets must be removed individually to their own warm (a constant 70 to 75°F), humid rearing containers such as margarine tubs, plastic shoe boxes, or small aquaria that have a moist layer of shredded sphagnum moss, a few small pieces of tree bark, and a jam jar or coffee lid holding a wad of saturated tissue paper. Good ventilation must be provided. Initially these froglets are extremely delicate and troublesome to feed, and casualties will be inevitable. Hatchling crickets, hatchling waxworms, leaf lice/aphids/greenflies (ensure these have not been treated with pesticide), and springtails form the staple diet. If this can be offered regularly, frogs will grow to 12 to 15mm within six to eight weeks. During this stage they will begin to develop the adult coloration. They can gradually be offered larger food items and, if provided with the correct hygienic conditions, can be introduced into an adult setup within 6 to 14 months, when they will be sexually mature.

HEALTH AND DISEASE

Generally speaking, mantellas are very resistant to disease. This may be attributed to the alkaloid toxins (similar to those of dendrobatids) secreted through the skin. In addition, practicing good terrarium hygiene at all times will go a long way to ensuring that specimens remain in tip-top condition. The only likely occurrence of ailments is either when mantellas are first acquired, through mechanical injuries in easily stressed species, or when kept under incorrect conditions.

HEALTH REGIME FOR NEW ACQUISITIONS

The most likely ailments in newly acquired mantellas are stress and malnutrition. Generally speaking, mantellas travel quite well if properly packaged in warm moss-filled containers; however, they may dislike constantly being bumped around and will be quite stressed out when removed. Sometimes stress is not always so apparent, and to be safe they should always be transferred to clean containers half-filled with fresh damp moss and located in a warm (70 to 72°F), dark area. Initially a few fruitflies should be offered—if the frogs are not stressed they will feed immediately; if they ignore food, leave them a day or so before offering food again. All mantellas

A fungal spore taken from a growth on an infected frog. Fungal infections sometimes appear in frogs kept in moist surroundings where there is too little ventilation.

PHOTO: E. ELKAN.

A male Bernhard's Mantella, *Mantella bernhardi.* The yellow leg bases may serve as flash colors that when suddenly exposed divert the attention of a predator for a few seconds as the frog escapes. They also may serve as species recognition patterns for these frogs, which usually are found in dark areas on the forest floor.

Photo: M. Staniszewski.

should remain in such a location for about four to seven days and should never be introduced immediately into an existing colony. This is known as quarantining and gives the hobbyist the opportunity to assess the health of the new specimens. Introducing parasite-loaded frogs into a healthy colony is a recipe for disaster! Malnutrition unfortunately is quite common in wild-caught mantellas, which may be in transit for several weeks without food. It is during such a journey that disease is most likely to strike, therefore making the initial quarantine period doubly essential. At first the starved mantellas will appear in a dull, lethargic condition and even refuse food for the first few days. I know from experience that if they are given warm, humid, and shady conditions they soon will settle down and begin to avidly take fruitflies and small crickets liberally dusted in a multivitamin powder. Avoid feeding small waxworm larvae at this stage because, due to the elastic skin, they invariably will be regurgitated, further expending the mantella's limited energy resources. If newly acquired mantellas still refuse food after a few days, then the trick is to bathe them several times daily in a shallow dish of warm water enriched with a combined multivitamin/mineral solution. This will be absorbed through the skin and can trigger the feeding behavior.

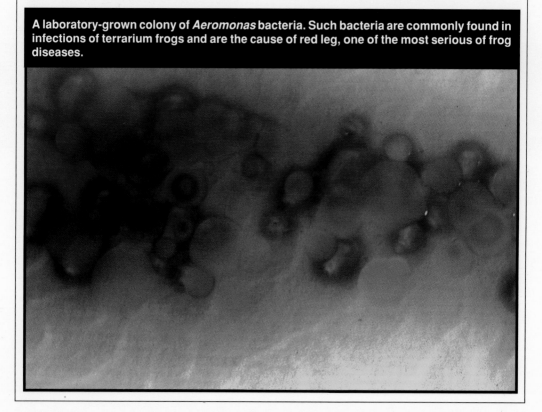

A laboratory-grown colony of *Aeromonas* bacteria. Such bacteria are commonly found in infections of terrarium frogs and are the cause of red leg, one of the most serious of frog diseases.

PHOTO: A. V. D. NIEUWENHUIZEN.

A belly view of *Mantella madagascariensis*, the Malagasy Mantella. The bright red legs and thighs of many species of this genus make an early diagnosis of red leg difficult or impossible.

SNOUT WOUNDS

Nervous species such as *M. pulchra* and *M. aurantiaca* "*milotympanum*"—particularly wild-caught specimens—often will attempt to leap through the clear glass of an aquarium or glass front of a wooden terrarium, sometimes sustaining snout or forelimb injuries. These would heal under normal conditions, but if such behavior persists the wounds can become progressively worse and infected. Treatment is with an effective broad-spectrum tropical fish bactericide by dissolving the suggested dosage in a pint of water and applying to the wound with a swab of soft cotton wool several times a day. Frogs can even be bathed in the solution for five to ten minutes twice a day where infection is particularly bad. The best method is preventative medicine, blocking off the glass when the mantellas are not being viewed, at least until they settle down in captivity.

RED LEG

Bearing in mind their small size, treatment for external and internal pathogens rarely cropping up in these frogs can prove very difficult. I have found in the past that simply applying those preparations sold for tropical fish at one and a half to twice the recommended strength for fish and bathing the specimen in this for five to ten minutes twice daily can prove successful. The only other disease I have witnessed in these frogs was on one occasion the infamous "red leg" caused by the bacterium *Aeromonas hydrophilia*. This can be very difficult to detect in its early stages in mantellas because the femoral glands around the cloaca and the orange to red thigh markings on many species may be mistaken for the characteristic suffusion of red or orange caused by this disease. If unsure, use a magnifying glass to closely study the "affected" area. A tiny network of ruptured capillaries spread across the surface of the thighs and ventral surface will be evident if red leg is rife. Fortunately red leg is extremely rare in mantellas. Treatment involves bathing the whole body of the frog in a 1% solution of copper sulfate, preferably in the form of the safer "chelated copper" products used by tropical fish hobbyists.

SHORT LIVES

The lifespan of some of the newly discovered mantellas is still very uncertain, but it is likely that they follow the same pattern as the more established species, depending on their climate/ habitat of origin. Generally speaking, those species originating from the cooler highlands of Madagascar are longer lived due to a slower metabolism. Lowland species such as *M. viridis*, *M. betsileo*, and *M. cowani* have an average life span of about five to seven years, while highland species such as *M. aurantiaca* and *M. pulchra* can attain ten years or more. I currently have a male Golden Mantella that has been in my collection for seven years, and it was acquired as a fully-grown adult. Obviously correct diet, suitable captive conditions, and correct hygiene will greatly increase a mantella's longevity.

THE SPECIES

Although the present taxonomy of mantellas is clearer than it has ever been, the validity of some species still is in question due to the complex nature of patterning, coloration, general appearance, and distribution of "species" in the wild; there also may be some natural hybridization. There currently are 11 named mantellas as well as a host of as yet undescribed types, the more distinct of which may later be given specific names or else merged into existing species once thorough geographical and biological research has been undertaken. It also is envisaged that new discoveries will be made in the next few years, particularly as the western regions of Madagascar remain largely unexplored. Two provisionally named mantella species have

A female Blue-legged Mantella, *Mantella expectata*, one of the most contrastingly patterned mantellas. Not discovered until 1991, it is found in a valley with remnant moist forest in the arid southwestern part of Madagascar near Toliara.
Photo: M. Staniszewski.

been included in the following descriptions as they are generally recognized as sufficiently distinct in appearance and behavior. In addition two subspecific forms of *Mantella aurantiaca*—subspecies *rubra* and the informally named subspecies *"milotympanum,"* have been described, but having maintained both types I would suggest that the latter be elevated to specific status because it is quite disparate from the Golden Mantella in size, appearance, disposition, and general behavior.

The named species can be divided into four groups based on their distribution, appearance, and habits, all of which have been available to hobbyists at some time or other particularly in recent years.

Coastal Mantellas (Mantella betsileo group)

These species occur in lowland and coastal regions of Madagascar and Reunion, often outside forests. Apart from some populations of *Mantella viridis*, the single red/orange blotch on each inner thigh distinctive of other mantellas generally is absent, and these species often exhibit a pale stripe on the upper lip.

- **Brown Mantella (Mantella betsileo)**

Perhaps one of the plainest of the mantellas, it still is sought after all the same. The general dorsal coloration ranges from a mustard-brown to copper, often with faint square or diamond-shaped markings. The flanks are well defined in black while the

The Brown Mantella, *Mantella betsileo*, is one of the plainest species of the genus. It also is one of the few that sometimes has a distinct pattern of brown lines within the back color.

Photo: P. Freed.

legs are marbled in dark gray and bluish gray. A white stripe is prominent around the upper lip. Attaining a length of 22 to 28mm, it is a medium sized species that occurs in small pockets throughout Madagascar but is particularly evident in the northern coastal regions. Males can be distinguished from females by a slightly more angular head, their highly territorial nature, and also a slight looseness in the skin of the throat.

In captivity it requires a humid terrarium with either a mossy or absorbent sponge base with plenty of broken crockery, pieces of bark, and a small shallow pool. Plants generally are not necessary, although leaves scattered over the basal substrate are good. Exclusively diurnal in habits, it is rather bold, with males in particular securing an elevated position to show off their calling skills for many hours each day. It has been bred only occasionally in captivity, with clutches in the 25 to 70 range usually being produced in May to August although sometimes throughout the year.

• **Green Mantella** *(Mantella viridis)*
Discovered as recently as 1988 in the Montagne de Francais region of the extreme northern tip of Madagascar, this is the largest known species of mantella, with females capable of attaining 35mm (although they usually measure around 30mm). Males are much smaller, rarely reaching 25mm. There possibly are two forms, one with a dorsal

A male Green Mantella, *Mantella viridis*. Notice the orange flash color hidden behind the knee.

Photo: M. Staniszewski.

PHOTO: M. STANISZEWSKI.

A female Green Mantella, *Mantella viridis*. Notice the orange under the thigh and that the black stripe on the side does not go into the groin.

can be seen as a yellow bulge through the flanks) they either rarely produce clutches or the deposited eggs remain unfertilized. Interference by both the keeper and other mantella species may be the cause of this although there is no clear evidence suggesting this is true. In the wild clutches consist of up to 45 small pale green eggs that take up to ten days to hatch, the incredibly strong tadpoles being able to squirm short distances to a water source if no flooding is prevalent.

- **Blue-legged Mantella** (*Mantella expectata*)
  One of the gems of the genus, this tiny species was first discovered in a small fertile valley near Toliara, the arid stretch of extreme southwestern Madagascar, in 1991 and subsequently was named the following year. Further discoveries were made in western (Isalo) and extreme southeastern (Mandena) Madagascar in 1993. Males attain 20 to 24mm and females 31mm, with both being handsomely adorned in a yellow or mustard dorsum with blackish flanks and distinctive slate gray to light or iridescent blue legs. A bluish lip line is also evident.
  So far very little is known about the habits of this species, although it is known to prefer slightly drier habitats than other species but must have access to a shallow body of water. Several shipments of this species have come out of Madagascar so far, but as yet no records of

coloration of a dirty brownish green gradually blending into darker flanks, the other a beautiful grass-green with well-defined flank markings, cream lip markings, and bright red blotches on the thighs. The latter "form" is generally smaller than the normal "form." The underside of both is black with blue or gray speckles.

In captivity this species prefers a rather open environment with plenty of hiding places. It tends to be active during the morning and around dusk, when it busily hunts for anything up to the size of a bluebottle fly (in fact, it is one of the least fussy mantellas where feeding is concerned). At other times the male seeks a concealed position from where he will spend hours calling with a voice that sounds very much like a cricket. Females are somewhat shyer, and although they regularly develop eggs throughout the year (which

A female Blue-legged Mantella, *Mantella expectata*.

successful breeding exist. Reports are that it adapts well to captivity but must be given a rainy season to stimulate courtship.

Golden Mantellas *(Mantella aurantiaca-group)*

This is essentially a highland group confined to the central-western hills and mountains around Andasibe and Moramanga, Madagascar. Therefore it is no surprise that it consists of the hardiest mantellas that thrive in captivity and regularly produce clutches of eggs. A red or orange blotch is present on the inner thigh of all species (although this can be difficult to detect in *M. aurantiaca*). All species possess aposematic colors warning of the fairly toxic alkaloids in the skin that are capable of stunning a small mammal and causing local discomfort in humans.

A male Golden Mantella, *Mantella aurantiaca aurantiaca*, of the typical form. This bright golden frog is the most familiar mantella.

- **Golden Mantella** *(Mantella aurantiaca)*

This is the most popular and conspicuously colored member of the genus. It occurs in several distinct color forms each restricted to their own small locality on Madagascar. The typical orange form is found around Andasibe, where it is synonymous with the humid *Pandanus* forests; the yellow form occurs in the virgin forests of Beparasay; and the red form is known from Anosibe An'Ala. All have huge, rather soulful black eyes. All three are found above 500m. The female generally is larger than the male, attaining 25mm while males rarely grow over 22mm. The color tends to be uniform although occasionally small dark spots are apparent in some individuals. Males can be determined by close inspection of the ventral surface, where the thin white lines of the seminiferous ducts are evident. Both sexes are territorial, often wrestling with individuals that encroach upon their territory. Males are not as vociferous as other mantellas, the call being a series of short low clicks.

The Golden Mantella prefers a cool (74°F maximum, preferably 70°F), humid terrarium with plenty of leaf litter, vantage points, and a shallow water source. The typical orange form and the red form (sometimes known as *M. a. rubra)* are extremely bold, while the yellow form is quite reticent. Females can produce up to 100 small white eggs that generally are deposited in moss or in a suitably damp depression. Unfortunately

Head-on view of a Golden Mantella, *Mantella aurantiaca rubra*. The subspecies of this mantella are rather poorly defined and based to a great extent just on color.

A male (above) and female of the red subspecies of the Golden Mantella, *Mantella aurantiaca rubra*. Females tend to be plumper than the stream-lined males.

males seem reluctant to fertilize clutches, which will spoil in three or four days. Fertilized eggs develop in two or three days and should be left *in situ* for two to seven days, at which point the tadpoles should be gently flooded into a water bowl and transferred to an aquarium. It has been witnessed for tadpoles to complete development within the gelatinous egg shell, with miniature frogs hatching out 45 to 55 days later; however, this is extremely rare and may only transpire in isolated high-altitude populations. Newly metamorphosed Golden Mantellas are 6 to 9mm long and are greenish brown in color. If reared individually or in groups of two to five and given a regular supply of aphids, small fruitflies, and hatchling Lesser Waxworms, mortality rate is quite low and

A male Black-eared Mantella, *Mantella aurantiaca "milotympanum."*

maturity is achieved within a year. Collection of these frogs in the wild is now strictly controlled as the small populations are in danger of extinction. It has just been placed on the CITES list.

The **Black-eared Mantella (*Mantella aurantiaca "milotympanum"*)** is much smaller than typical *M.*

The Black-eared Mantella is a so-far undescribed form. It probably represents a full species, not just a subspecies of *aurantiaca.*

aurantiaca, attaining just 15 to 18mm. Both sexes are identical in size and coloration, but males possess a somewhat greener ventral surface. The uniform coloring is a deep or rusty orange; the specific name is derived from the black tympanum. Occurring in the Fiherenana Valley, it is an extremely shy species—an attribute that meant it was not discovered until 1993. The male is among the most vociferous of all mantellas, and although breeding has not yet been documented in captivity, the ease with which this species can be maintained and the seeming willingness of males to mate may mean this should not prove too difficult in the future.

• **Yellow Mantella (*Mantella crocea*)**
Occurring at an altitude of 500 to 1000m in the hills of Andasibe and Moramanga, western Madagascar, this mantella ranges from greenish brown or dirty orange to a stunning lemon and black speckled form that may eventually be split into a separate species. In the typical form

PHOTO: M. STANISZEWSKI.

This male Yellow Mantella, *Mantella crocea*, belongs to the black-specked form.

indistinct reticulations are present on the dorsum, while the legs, flanks, and lower part of the head are black or dark brown. Males attain 20mm while females can reach 25mm; this is quite a plump species. The venter usually is black with bluish markings, although in the yellow individuals it is much lighter. Sexes can be determined in accordance with *M. aurantiaca*. This is the ideal species for the beginner as it does extremely well in captivity and is tolerant of cool conditions. It is a showy species and will breed regularly, with males in particular being very active and vociferous,

In the Yellow Mantella the black band on the side often extends into the groin.

PHOTO: M. STANISZEWSKI.

the call being lower than in most other species. Clutches of 25 to 70 pale brown eggs can be produced throughout the year, and fertilization rates are good at about 70% if a ratio of two males to every female is maintained. The eggs hatch out in 10 to 18 days and must be transferred to a shallow aquarium immediately.

PHOTO: K. H. SWITAK.

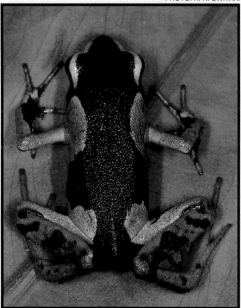

The symmetry of the pattern of the Malagasy Mantella, *Mantella madagascariensis*, sometimes is remarkable. The large colored spots at the bases of the legs are typical of the allies of this species.

Variegated Mantellas *(M. madagascariensis*-group)

These represent the most diverse mantellas in terms of geographical distribution, and most habitat types on Madagascar have been infiltrated by one or more of the species. The pretty harlequin patterns have made these extremely popular with terrarium keepers, and the recent discovery of two further species has further heightened the interest in variegated mantellas.

- **Malagasy Mantella** *(M. madagascariensis)*

This was the first mantella to be named way back in 1872 and it has the widest distribution of any species, being found throughout western Madagascar and even the island of Reunion. It is mainly a highland species often found in the 500- to 1200-m range, but populations in the south and on Reunion occur at sea level. Females are fairly large, growing to 32mm, while males usually are smaller than 25mm. The coloration and patterning are highly variable, with the dorsum, head, and front limbs being black broken by yellow or light green areas. A distinctive light yellow or white rostral stripe runs over each eye, while the legs usually are stunningly colored in orange or red with black striations. The belly and throat are black with a few greenish or gray spots. The colors are a sign of its potent skin toxins that can cause local swellings in humans and death in small mammals and snakes. A very vigorous, showy species in captivity, males in particular emit a loud clicking noise when excited. Males are not as territorial as are those of other species. It nearly always is found in the vicinity of water, therefore the terrarium should be furnished accordingly.

The contrast in color between the greenish or yellowish thigh and orange lower leg is normal in *Mantella madagascariensis*. This is a beautifully marked adult female from Andasibe.

PHOTO: M. STANISZEWSKI

Preferred temperatures depend on the exact location, those from high altitudes requiring a cooler 65 to 72°F while lowland types prefer 72 to 78°F. Clutches are small, usually containing 20 to 30 white eggs 2mm in diameter. Hatching, development, and metamorphosis are the longest of the known mantella species, often taking 65 to 70 days to complete. Froglets are quite large at 10 to 12mm and are a grayish color with few markings. Adult coloration can be seen after 30 to 50 days.

Mantella "loppei" from Beparasy, eastern Madagascar, is very similar to *M. madagascariensis* but it differs in

PHOTO: R. D. BARTLETT.

An odd mantella agreeing with the form called *Mantella "loppei"* by hobbyists. This and several other unusual mantellas probably represent undescribed species.

the dorsum displaying an intricate network of fine yellow spots or reticulations, completely orange inner thigh coloring, granular reddish femoral glands, and a white horseshoe shape on the throat. The ventral color is green or bluish rather than black.

PHOTO: M. STANISZEWSKI.

The exact identity of this black and orange mantella is still disputed, but currently it is called *Mantella cowani*, the Variegated or Painted Mantella. The large orange leg spots are distinctive.

- **Variegated Mantella** *(Mantella cowani)*

After the Golden Mantella *(M. aurantiaca)* this beautiful little species from the highlands (around 900m) east of Betsileo, Antoetra, and Fianarantosa in central-west Madagascar is the most popular terrarium subject. Until recently most specimens sold under this name actually were color varieties of *Mantella madagascariensis*, but it now is known that the true *M. cowani* is fairly constant in coloration. A number of small orange-red or orange-yellow blotches or bands are present around the front arm pits and along the hind limbs. The rest of the dorsum, the head, and the flanks are uniformly black, rarely exhibiting small orange, red, or yellow bars on the tibia and tarsus. The digits are always black, and the inner arms and underside regularly show white blotches. As with the preceding species, with which it is known to hybridize where populations overlap, its skin also contains

PHOTO: P. FREED.

Whether *Mantella cowani* is a full species or just a subspecies or color morph of *Mantella madagascariensis* remains uncertain. The two are known to hybridize when they come into contact.

toxic alkaloid secretions. Males are smaller at about 25mm, while females are about 27 to 28mm. It has been bred regularly in captivity, and it appears that a small, rather than spacious, terrarium is likely to give more success as regular interaction between the sexes is required for a successful pairing. It is a very shy species, and although males call regularly this is always from beneath leaf litter. Egg clutches range from 15 to 50 eggs that are quick to develop. Unfortunately the tadpoles are difficult to maintain, although I have found that very shallow water (1 to 2 inches) that is richly oxygenated and at a temperature no greater than 68°F proves successful. Froglets are very small at 6mm and can be troublesome to feed. However, if you manage to keep them going for the first six to eight weeks, they gradually become stronger and quite vigorous, with maturity being attained in just six months.

- **Beautiful Mantella (*Mantella pulchra)***

This is a "large" non-poisonous mantella that can be confused with the toxic *M. madagascariensis*, of which it is a mimic. Its coloring and patterning are known as protective or Batesian mimicry and warn potential predators from attacking it. It can easily be distinguished from *M. madagascariensis* by the brownish sheen to the head and dorsum. The flanks and insertion of the hind limbs usually have a lime green, emerald, or blue patch, and a large red to orange blotch is present on each inner thigh. The belly is black with tiny bluish flecks. The head is quite angular, and overall this is a rather plump species. It is basically a highland species from Andasibe. Both sexes attain 30mm, with females being rather more plump but otherwise difficult to determine.

In captivity it prefers plenty of humid hiding places as it is an extremely nervous species. Males rarely call in captivity, but when they do it is a rapid double click at two- or three-second intervals.

This male Beautiful Mantella, *Mantella pulchra*, is not displaying the brilliant leg colors.

PHOTO: M. STANISZEWSKI

Breeding currently is unknown in captivity, although isolation of this species from other mantella species

PHOTO: M. STANISZEWSKI.

In the right light and with the legs open to show the flash colors, the Beautiful Mantella really is a beautiful frog.

appears to be essential even where courtship is concerned.

- **Haraldmeier's Mantella** *(Mantella haraldmeieri)*

A rare variegated species described in 1981 and known only from four locations in Tolagnaro in the extreme south-east of Madagascar. Females can reach 28mm, while males rarely grow to 23mm. In shape it is very similar to *Mantella pulchra* but is slightly more slender in build. The dorsum generally is bronzy, often with an inverted dark Y or V shape roughly in line with the front limbs. The flanks usually are black, although the specimens I saw had gray flanks. Perhaps the most conspicuous characteristic is the pale blue to lime-green upper front limbs. The venter is black with blue speckles, while the insides of the legs usually are a flesh to red color. Haraldmeier's Mantella is said to lay about 65 eggs in a 25-

mm diameter ball placed in damp leaf liter. The eggs are quite yellow in appearance, and it is thought that development may sometimes take place entirely within the egg capsule, as the eggs are often deposited far from water. Perhaps only four to six tadpoles will develop, utilizing the gelatinous ball and other embryos as nourishment. Such behavior has been noted in other species. Juveniles are about 10mm on metamorphosis, which is

ART BY J. QUINN.

Haraldmeier's Mantella, *Mantella haraldmeieri*, remains one of the most poorly known and least available of the mantellas.

relatively quite large. Coloration is immediately comparable to that of the adults.

- **Bernhard's Mantella** *(Mantella bernhardi)*

This is the most recent addition to the subfamily Mantellinae, having been discovered as recently as 1994, and what a gem it is! The general dorsal color is a silky black often with a faint gold vertebral stripe. The upper fore- and hind limbs are a dazzling

PHOTO: M. STANISZEWSKI.

A male Bernhard's Mantella, *Mantella bernhardi*. This species was described only in 1994.

days later they were about 10mm long and light gray. Thereafter growth was very slow (regardless of temperature). They were fed on a diet of shredded moss and powdered fish flakes. A hundred days later the first froglet (completely black in color) metamorphosed. Some tadpoles still are developing almost 200 days later and measure just 20mm, representing by far the slowest development of mantelline tadpoles. In the wild, clutches of

PHOTO: M. STANISZEWSKI.

Though not especially colorful, Bernhard's Mantella appeals to the specialist because of its rarity and novelty.

yellow, and the lower limbs are reticulated in reddish brown and black. The venter is black with many bluish speckles. Males and females are identical in size, attaining only 18 to 22mm, so the best way of identifying them is the whitish blue horseshoe-shaped band on the throat that is more extended on males and quite small or even absent in females. Initially in captivity it may refuse food for up to a week, but if given a spacious, humid terrarium and offered a mixture of crickets, fruitflies, and aphids it quickly will settle down. Both sexes are very showy, with males seeking elevated locations where they will raise their body off the ground and inflate their vocal sac. The cricket-like call is the loudest of any mantella species and certainly is different from any other species. I bred this species for the first time in August, 1995. Eggs were small and white, and embryo development was rapid. The unpigmented 5-mm tadpoles wriggled out into a shallow water dish after just three days. Ten

15 to 30 small white eggs usually are deposited in damp, rotting wood that eventually is flooded with rain. It is one of the few species to remain active for a few hours after dusk when calling intensifies.

A froglet of *Mantella bernhardi* displays the species-specific forearm coloration and pattern though the rest of the pattern is much paler than that of the adult.

PHOTO: M. STANISZEWSKI.

Climbing Mantellas *(Mantella laevigata-group)*

These are the most divergent of the mantellas in terms of morphology, behavior, and habitat and represent the most demanding in captivity due to the specialized setup required.

- ### Climbing Mantella *(Mantella laevigata)*

Found in the northeastern forests of Madagascar, this is the most arboreal mantella, although it still is largely terrestrial. Males are about 24mm, while females can attain 28 to 30mm. The head and upper dorsum range from a coppery green to yellow, while the limbs, flanks, and lower head are black, often with minute green speckles. The fingertips are greatly enlarged to act as suckers when scaling rocks and trees. The venter is black with a few white spots, and the throat is devoid of spots.

In captivity it requires a tall humid terrarium heated to around 76°F maximum with either a thick branch containing hollow, damp, moss-lined cavities or sections of sloping hollow, damp, moss-lined bamboo. Here Climbing Mantellas will retire during nighttime. It is a shy species, and calling in males rarely is heard. However, amplexus can regularly be seen in captivity. The white eggs (2.5mm in diameter) are attached singly to the outside of the branch or bamboo so that when the tadpoles emerge 8 to 12 days later they will fall into water. A total of 12 to 25 eggs is deposited in this fashion. The water dish must be located so it can accept the falling tadpoles. Sometimes

PHOTO: M. STANISZEWSKI.

The greatly expanded toe pads of the Climbing Mantella, *Mantella laevigata*, are distinctive in the genus, as is the greatly contrasting color pattern.

eggs are laid within the hollows, which in nature are then flooded with rainwater. Tadpole development takes place entirely within these hollows. Breeding has been accomplished regularly in captivity, but this species is not common in mantella collections due to its rather secretive nature in the wild.

The **Marojezy Mantella (Mantella "marojezi")** is very similar in appearance and size to the Climbing Mantella. It is completely terrestrial and can be distinguished by its brown- and black-banded limbs, speckles on the dorsum, and narrow white lip line. The throat also has a blue horseshoe-shaped marking that can be used in differentiating the sexes as in *M. bernhardi*. It has only just been made available to hobbyists but often is misnamed *M. laevigata*. It requires much cooler conditions than *M. laevigata* as it occurs 500 to 1300m up in the Marojezy Mountains. A maximum of 72°F is advised, along with plenty of humid hiding places and a canopy of plants. Breeding behavior currently is unknown.

THE GENUS *MANTIDACTYLUS*

The other half of the subfamily Mantellinae is the huge yet largely unknown genus called *Mantidactylus*. There currently are 55 to 60 named species divided into ten species groups based upon morphology, geographical distribution, behavior, and reproductive modes. Many species are truly arboreal, often to the extent that they rarely venture to the forest floor, while others are terrestrial and share many similarities with mantellas both in behavior and reproductive cycles. Of the arboreal types most are within the 18- to 35-mm range and rather plain in coloration (usually brown to dark gray); in common with other Madagascan anurans they are largely diurnal and therefore make excellent captives. *Mantidactylus liber* and *M. wittei* are the species most likely to be seen in captivity and require tall humid terraria with a number of

PHOTO: W. P. MARA.

Mantidactylus pulcher is one of the smaller and more delicate species of the genus. Few species are this attractive.

branches and plants. The most beautiful of the arboreal mantidactylas is the diminutive *M. grandisonae*, which possesses ivory flanks and underside and reddish arms. Like many arboreal mantidactylas, females attach their gelatinous clumps of 50 to 150 eggs about half a meter above the water.

Ground-dwelling mantidactylas show a wide divergence in size and appearance. *Mantidactylus kely* measures just 15mm, while the voracious, stockily built *M. guttulatus* attains 12cm. Many species occur in high-altitude cool forests, and thus such conditions must apply in captivity. The 4-cm *M. betsileanus* is one of the most common Malagasy frogs and occasionally is exported. *M. albofrenatus* is very similar to *Mantella betsileo* in appearance, habits, and reproductive habits; this is thought to be a case of Batesian mimicry.

Mantidactylus webbi, one of the many seldom-available Madagascan mantidactylas.

PHOTO: P. FREED.

PHOTO: P. FREED.

***Mantidactylus flavobrunneus*, one of the less colorful members of the genus. Notice the greatly enlarged toe pads of this and most species of the genus.**

Some mantidactylas show other types of mimicry such as crypsis (breakdown of the outline to merge in with the background). The 3- to 4-cm partly-arboreal *Mantidactylus cornutus*—the Madagascan Horned Frog—from Andasibe is a wonderful example of this, displaying an array of dermal spines and horns that make it virtually invisible against the bark of trees.

An unidentified *Mantidactylus*. The delicate lime coloration of the jaws and throat is an interesting feature of this species.

PHOTO: R. D. BARTLETT.

Another view of *Mantidactylus* sp. from the previous page. Distinguishing unidentified mantidactyla imports from some treefrogs could be very difficult.

Photo: R. D. Bartlett.